Heinz Nordhoff, architect of the Beetle's astounding post-war success, in front of the Volkswagen factory at Wolfsburg in July 1953. This is one of a series of photographs taken for a cover of 'Time' magazine. Eventually a drawing was used instead.

THE VOLKSWAGEN BEETLE

Jonathan Wood

Shire Publications Ltd

CONTENTS

Published in 2003 by Shire Publications Ltd, Cromwell House, Church Street, Princes Risborough, Buckinghamshire HP27 9AA, UK. Copyright © 1989 and 2003 by Jonathan Wood. First published 1989; reprinted 1993. Second edition 2003. Shire Album 226. ISBN 0 7478 0565 2.

Printed in Great Britain by CIT Printing Services Ltd, Press Buildings, Merlins Bridge, Haverfordwest, Pembrokeshire SA61 1XF.

British Library Cataloguing in Publication Data: Wood, Jonathan. The Volkswagen Beetle. 1. The Volkswagen. Beetle cars, history. I. Title. 629. 2'222.
ISBN 0 7478 0565 2.

Editorial Consultant: Michael E. Ware, former Director of the National Motor Museum, Beaulieu.

ACKNOWLEDGEMENTS
The author gratefully acknowledges the assistance of Volkswagenwerke AG, VAG (United Kingdom) Limited and Dr Ing h. c. F. Porsche AG in the preparation of this book. Illustrations are acknowledged as follows: Imperial War Museum, London, page 10; National Motor Museum, cover; Volkswagen do Brasil, page 27 (bottom); VW-Fotozentrale, pages 11 (bottom), 12. Other illustrations are from the author's collection.

Cover: *A 1953 Volkswagen Beetle Export G model.*

Below: *The origins of the Volkswagen shape can be seen in this 1932 experimental Wanderer, which never entered production and was used by Porsche as his personal transport. It is photographed in front of his Stuttgart house; the first experimental Volkswagens were built in the double garage behind.*

The Wanderer's lines were scaled down for another experimental Porsche, designated Type 12, which the design bureau produced for the Zündapp motorcycle company. It had a backbone chassis, all-independent suspension and a rear-mounted engine, though this had five cylinders.

HITLER, PORSCHE AND THE *KDF-WAGEN*

When the Berlin Motor Show opened in February 1939, visitors had their first opportunity to examine the *KdF-Wagen*, or what we know today as the Volkswagen Beetle. Relaunched after the Second World War, it has become the most popular car ever made, the 21 millionth having been built in 1992.

How did this unconventional and individual car, known throughout the world as the Beetle or the Bug, come to be built? The idea came from Adolf Hitler, leader of the Munich-based National Socialist party, who in 1924 was imprisoned in Landsberg Castle, following an unsuccessful putsch on the Federal German capital. Hitler conceived an idea to solve Germany's unemployment problems. The government would build special motor roads, like the Italian autostradas created by Benito Mussolini, his fascist contemporary. He envisaged a Nazi state mass-producing a small car at a price within the reach of the man in the street – the Volkswagen. Here Hitler was undoubtedly inspired by the success of the Model T Ford, at the time the most popular car in the world.

Just under a decade later, in February 1933, Hitler and the Nazis swept to power in Germany, and at his first cabinet meeting Hitler raised the matter of motor roads. In September of the same year work began on a network of concrete dual carriageways. By 1943 there were 2380 miles (3827 km) of these autobahns in Germany. The matter of the People's Car took longer to resolve, however, the design not being finalised until 1938. The car made its debut in 1939, but the outbreak of the Second World War ensured that it never entered series production during the twelve years of the Third Reich.

The contract for this important project was awarded, in April 1934, to the Stuttgart-based Porsche design bureau. It was given ten months to complete the work. The renowned Austrian engineer Ferdinand Porsche and his design team had a difficult job initially in meeting Hitler's design parameters. The car must have a top speed of 62 mph (100 km/h) and a petrol consumption of 42 miles per gallon (7 litres per 100 km); it must have an air-cooled engine and be able to carry two adults and three children. Perhaps the most stringent stipulation was that it should sell for no more than 1000 *Reichsmarks* (£86).

Ferdinand Porsche (1875-1951), the distinguished Austrian engineer and 'father' of the Volkswagen, who had set up a design bureau in Stuttgart in 1930, pictured in 1938 at the height of his powers.

It was for this last reason that Porsche opted for a rear-mounted engine for the design identified as Type 60 in his bureau register. He had already produced an experimental 1.2 litre rear-engined car for the Zündapp motorcycle company in 1931. However, his starting point for the Type 60 was a 1933 derivative produced for NSU, another motorcycle manufacturer. That design embodied a 1.5 litre horizontally opposed air-cooled engine (known as a boxermotor in Germany), but its four cylinders were unsatisfactory, probably on cost grounds. Porsche experimented with vertical four-cylinder and then with two-cylinder sleeve-valve and overhead-valve boxermotors, but none proved satisfactory. The problem was solved when, in 1935, Franz Xaver Reimspiess, an Austrian engineer who had joined the team only the previous year, produced a design for a 984 cc, four-cylinder boxermotor, after spending only two days working on it. When costed by Porsche's estimator, Oswald Kux, it

was found to be cheaper to produce than the two-cylinder engines then under development. Enlarged to 985 cc by 1938, basically the same engine has powered over 20 million Volkswagens.

The Type 60 featured a backbone chassis, a popular central European feature of its day inspired by the Czechoslovakian Type 11 Tracta of 1923. The idea of all-independent suspension came from the same source, though the Type 60 used simple and ingenious torsion bars patented by Porsche in 1931, with a cheap swing-axle layout at the rear. The car's distinctive bodywork lines can be traced back to a 3.5 litre saloon Porsche designed for Wanderer in 1931, refined for the Zündapp and NSU projects. However, Hitler took a personal interest in the appearance of the car, which also reflected the current German preoccupation with aerodynamics. 'It should look like a Beetle', insisted the Führer; 'you have to look to nature to find out what streamlining is.'

With the design finalised by 1938, a factory had to be built to manufacture the car. A site was chosen in northern Germany, on the bank of the Mitteland Canal, which joins the rivers Rhine and Elbe. Near the village of Fallersleben, it was 50 miles (80 km) east of Hanover. Hitler laid the foundation stone in May 1938, when he announced that the previously named Volkswagen would henceforth be known as the *KdF-Wagen* (Strength through Joy Car), named after the Nazi party's leisure section. The town that would be built to house the factory workers would be called *KdF-Stadt* (Strength through Joy Town). In August, the head of the German Labour Front, Robert Ley, announced that the basic *KdF* saloon, finished in blue-grey, would cost RM990 (£85), while a version with a roll-back sunroof was to cost another RM 60 (£5). However, instead of being sold in the usual way, the *KdF-Wagens* could only be bought in instalments, with the product available at the completion of payments rather than at the outset. A savings book costing RM1 would be issued, and this in effect placed an order for a car, and savings stamps could then be purchased. By the end of 1938 the Labour Front had received 167,741 ap-

4

In 1934 came this Type 32 project for NSU, regarded as the prototype for the Volkswagen. It had a backbone chassis, all-independent torsion-bar suspension and rear-mounted, air-cooled 1.5 litre engine.

When Porsche began work on the Volkswagen in 1934, he used the Type 32, with its rather blunt nose, as his starting point. It resulted in this sketch by Adolf Hitler, who wanted a more pointed front, and Porsche modified the design accordingly.

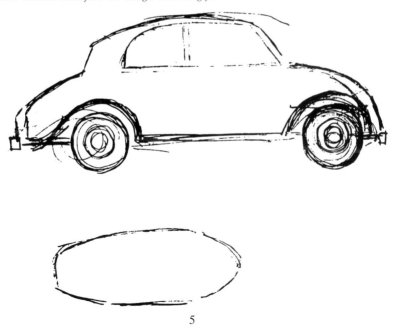

Porsche did not perpetuate the four-cylinder air-cooled engine used by the Type 32 because of the stringent RM1000 (£86) price ceiling. Instead, he developed a number of experimental two-cylinder engines, of which this is one, but it was replaced by a four-cylinder unit in 1936.

Three experimental Volkswagens, coded the VW3 series, were built in 1936. This example is pictured in the garden of Porsche's house, having been built in the garage there. This example has forward-opening doors and no rear window, both features which did not survive.

This is one of thirty experimental Volkswagens, built by Daimler-Benz in 1937 and submitted to a rigorous 50,000 mile (80,000 km) testing programme. Note that the headlamps are contained within the front wings and the modifications to the bonnet. Below is a rear view of the same series.

Hitler decreed that the car should 'look like a beetle. You have to look to nature to find out what streamlining is.' The VW30 achieved this. Note that there is still no rear window, with the three-tiered louvres demanded by the rear-mounted, air-cooled engine.

Adolf Hitler, with Ferdinand Porsche (back to camera), inspecting the car that he had just announced would be called the KdF-Wagen. The date is 26th May 1938 and the occasion his ceremonial laying of the factory's foundation stone. The Führer was subsequently driven, in a KdF-Wagen, to the nearby Fallersleben railway station by Ferdinand Porsche's son, Ferry.

The Volkswagen, as completed in 1938, ready for manufacture. These are pre-production cars which featured a new rear window and smaller engine-cooling louvres. The press was given the opportunity to drive them in the spring of 1939. They are pictured here at the hill near the Porsche headquarters overlooking the construction of the Volkswagen factory. The version with the cloth sunroof, on the extreme left, cost RM1050 (£90) and was RM60 (£5) more than the basic model.

The engine of the VW38 was a model of simplicity. The carburettor was a Solex unit while the dynamo on the top of the engine is a Bosch component. Its four cylinders are out of sight but the casing for the all-important cooling fan can be seen at the back of the engine.

plications, and the eventual figure rose to 336,668.

By the spring of 1939 the *KdF-Wagen* factory was capable of producing 150,000 cars a year, making it the largest car factory in Europe. But there were plans for an expansion, which would have resulted in increasing the capacity of the plant to 1.5 million cars *per annum* by 1942, when it would have rivalled the giants of Detroit. On 1st September 1939, however, the German army invaded Poland, the Second World War began, and although a small pilot run of *KdF-Wagens* began in 1941, only 630 cars were built during the war. These mostly went to high-ranking Nazis, including Adolf Hitler. The German public would have to wait until after the war to sample the pleasures of Volkswagen motoring.

The military version of the KdF-Wagen, the Kübelwagen, was produced from 1940 until the end of the Second World War. An example is seen here, with General Reichelt in the rear seat, under British supervision at the end of the war.

PLOUGHSHARES INTO SWORDS

When war began the Volkswagen factory was transferred from the German Labour Front to the Air Ministry and was soon servicing Junkers JU88 aircraft and maufacturing BMW aero-engines. Nevertheless, in February 1940, a Volkswagen of sorts began leaving the production lines. This was the *KdF-Wagen*-based military *Kübelwagen*, the German equivalent of the Allied Jeep.

When the Porsche company was contracted to develop the Volkswagen in 1934, the German government stipulated that it should also be capable of carrying three men, a machine-gun and ammunition. In 1937 one of the experimental cars was crudely modified to meet these requirements and this evolved into the doorless Type 62 of 1938. It was later refined, with angular bodywork and doors, and in 1939 saw service in Poland, the first theatre of war. There it was found that its lowest speed, 5 mph (8 km/h), was still too fast; what was required was the walking pace of a soldier with a full pack.

Ferdinand Porsche's son, Ferry, clever-

ly resolved the problem by introducing a reduction gear to each rear hub and lowering the front stub axles. This meant that the *KdF-Wagen* engine and gearbox could be retained intact, and at the same time the ground clearance of the *Kübelwagen* was raised, making it ideal for cross-country use in muddy and rutted conditions.

The air-cooled *Kübelwagen* proved its worth from the sands of the Sahara to the sub-zero temperatures of the Russian front. Although the Germans were fighting a global war, *Kübelwagen* production was relatively modest, with 50,435 vehicles built, compared with 585,000 Jeeps.

Porsche also developed an amphibious derivative. Designated Type 166, the *Schimmwagen* of 1942 was a relatively sophisticated vehicle with a five-speed gearbox; four-wheel drive engaged when the fifth cog was selected. It was capable of 50 mph (80 km/h) on land and 6 mph (10 km/h) in water. When used in this latter role, a member of the crew would manually lower a retractable propeller which then engaged with a dog clutch

10

The interior of the Kübelwagen, with the backbone chassis clearly visible. Note the petrol tank, with the filler adjoining the spare wheel. The oblong covers on the instrument panel are easily accessible fuse boxes, while the KdF-Wagen steering wheel is used unchanged.

Although some KdF-Wagens were produced during the war, none reached the public. However, the Kommandeurwagen of 1942 was a combination of the high Kübelwagen chassis, with four-wheel drive, and a KdF-Wagen saloon body. Introduced in 1942, only 667 were built during the war; a further two were made from spare parts in September 1946; this is one of them.

11

The Schimmwagen, an amphibious version of the KdF-Wagen, was introduced in 1942. Like the Kommandeurwagen, it featured four-wheel drive and when it took on its aquatic role the rear-mounted propeller, just visible, was manually lowered by detaching a clip from the rear silencer.

attached to a take-off from the rear-mounted engine. Just as the definitive *Kübelwagen* evolved from the Type 62 to the Type 82, so its amphibious equivalent developed from the Type 128 prototype of 1940 into the smaller Type 166. This was powered by an enlarged 1131 cc engine, with capacity increased from 985 cc by increasing the bore from 70 to 75 mm. This power unit was also fitted to the *Kübelwagen* from the following year. But the *Schimmwagen* was relatively scarce, only 14,283 being produced at the *KdF-Stadt* factory and by Porsche in Stuttgart between 1942 and 1945.

Despite the war, the Porsche bureau continued to refine the Volkswagen

design. Types 151 and 152 developed special transmission systems, 160 was a *KdF-Wagen* with unitary bodywork, 179 was a fuel-injection system for the Volkswagen engine, 225 dealt with electric transmission, while Type 298 was a radio receiver for the car. Porsche even used half a *KdF-Wagen* engine to actuate the auxiliaries of *Maus*, his extraordinary 185-ton mobile blockhouse, of which only two examples were built.

In the north, the vulnerable *KdF-Wagen* factory was attacked from April 1944 by the American Eighth Air Force, and three-quarters was destroyed by the time the war in Europe ended in May 1945.

In March 1946 production at the Volkswagen factory surpassed 1000 a month for the first time. Major Ivan Hirst of the Royal Electrical and Mechanical Engineers, who ran the Volkswagen factory from 1945 to 1947, is shown at the wheel of the thousandth Volkswagen, built that month. Note that the British were having to use conventional headlamps as the correct lenses were not available.

WORLD WAR TO WORLD CAR

When the Allies occupied Germany, *KdF-Stadt* was renamed Wolfsburg after a nearby fourteenth-century castle. The plant fell within the British military zone and in July 1945 the 30 Workshop Control Unit of the Royal Electrical and Mechanical Engineers was established at the plant, under the command of Major Ivan Hirst. *Kübelwagen* production had restarted in June, though the saloon, by then renamed the Volkswagen, did not begin until December. It soon overtook the *Kübelwagen*, which was merely being assembled from spare parts that were almost used up by the end of 1945. Hirst received an order for ten thousand cars for the British army, and this kept the Wolfsburg production lines running.

These early post-war Beetles were crude, noisy and badly finished, which was not surprising in view of the condi-tions in which Hirst and his team were operating. The 1131 cc engine, introduced in 1943, was still used, though the British Humber company, which tested one, found it was capable of only 56 mph (90 km/h), while their own Hillman Minx could achieve 61 mph (98 km/h).

An impressive 7677 Volkswagens were built in 1946 and output rose to 8987 in the following year, despite a severe winter. Then in the autumn of 1947 Hirst, supported by his immediate superior, Colonel Charles Radclyffe, appointed 48-year-old Heinz Nordhoff as general manager of Volkswagen and he took up his post on 1st January 1948. A former director of General Motors' German subsidiary Opel, Nordhoff had visited America before the war and was well versed in transatlantic mass-production methods.

Heinz Nordhoff's Export model of 1949. Unlike the standard car that continued in production for the home market, it was notable for its chrome trim, new grooved bumpers and hub caps. The horn, hitherto external, was positioned behind a small grille in one wing. The grille in the other wing was purely decorative.

During 1948, still operating under British supervision, Volkswagen built a record 19,244 cars. In September of the following year, the British presence was withdrawn. Nordhoff took complete control, while the ownership of the Volkswagen company was vested in the state of Lower Saxony, where Wolfsburg was located, acting as agents for the newly created German Federal Republic.

Once in charge, Nordhoff took two decisions that were to ensure the Volkswagen would become the most popular car in the world. The first was to establish a one-model policy, which echoed Henry Ford's strategy with the Model T forty years previously. The second was to retain the unconventional appearance of the Beetle. 'Professor Porsche had worked something into it that made this diamond very much worth our while polishing,' said Nordhoff, yet he was the first to recognise that the car needed a great deal of refinement. Nordhoff thus committed himself to a policy of improvement rather than revolution. Consequently, in 1981 it was calculated that the only one of the Beetle's 5115 parts in common with its 1945 predecessor was the rubber strip sealing the bonnet!

Nordhoff's prime objective was to develop the Volkswagen and transform it into a more acceptable vehicle that could be sold on the world market as well as in Germany. One reason why it was to prove so successful was that the Beetle was just the type of reliable, classless vehicle sought by the car-hungry post-war public. Building on this success, the process of refinement continued year by year and this, coupled with the excellent finish and outstanding reliability, ensured that the air-cooled Beetle was as popular in the snows of Canada as in the sweltering heat of the Brazilian summer.

The Export Volkswagen, which appeared in 1949, was instantly identifiable by its improved paintwork and chrome trim. Its grooved bumpers were also new and there were other minor improvements to the exterior. At the same time the interior was also improved, including a modernised dashboard, a new steering wheel, better finished upholstery and more comfortable seats.

Offered simultaneously with the Export Beetle were two factory-approved cabriolet (open) variants. Karmann of Osnabruck produced a four-seater convertible Beetle, which had modifications and improvements like the Export car.

Modifications were also made to the interior of the Export model. A new dark-faced speedometer, with ivory surround, was introduced, as was the optional mechanical clock, though both were contained within the old KdF-Wagen dashboard.

The Hebmuller two-seater cabriolet was a factory-approved variant which appeared in 1949. The majority were built during that year and in 1950, though a few cars continued to be made until 1953.

The four-seater Beetle cabriolet, built by Karmann between 1949 and 1980, and always the first to include Beetle improvements. This is a 1303 cabriolet, introduced in 1973, so perpetuating the MacPherson-strut independent suspension, five years after the saloon version had been discontinued.

The Karmann Ghia Volkswagen, based on the Export chassis, was introduced in 1955. This is the right-hand drive version, which arrived in 1960. The model lasted until 1974.

The Karmann Ghia coupé was joined by a cabriolet version for 1958. This is a 1960 model car, when the front air intakes were enlarged and the headlights raised.

This model was to be offered throughout the German saloon's manufacturing life and, indeed, outlasted it by two years, being made until 1980.

The other, shorter-lived variant came from the Wulfrath-based Hebmuller company, which offered a two-seater convertible Volkswagen with the folded hood taking up much of the space previously occupied by rear passengers. This proved less popular, the Hebmuller company being bankrupted in 1952, and the last few cars were finished by Karmann in 1953. Total production is estimated at about 750 cars, so the Hebmuller is much sought by collectors.

In March 1953 came the first significant modification to the Beetle's appearance when the central rib of the rear window, introduced in 1938, was removed, greatly improving the driver's view. In the following year the first alteration was made to the engine since the enlargement of 1942. Its bore size was enlarged from 75 to 77 mm, which increased capacity from 1131 to 1192 cc. Although the top speed of 62 mph (100 km/h) remained the same, acceleration was marginally improved.

The split rear window lasted only until March 1953, when the central rib was removed to improve the driver's view. This is a 1956 car, on which the single exhaust was replaced by twin pipes.

The rear of the Beetle received further refinement for 1958, when the oval rear window of 1953 was replaced by a much enlarged one, which also resulted in the cooling louvres being reduced in size. Changes were also made to the engine-lid moulding.

17

Demand for the Beetle continued to increase. In 1946 Volkswagen had become Germany's largest car maker, a position it has held ever since. Such was the car's popularity, both at home and abroad, that the millionth Beetle, with headlamps ablaze, left the Wolfsburg production line in August 1955.

The design continued to evolve. There was a further external change in 1958, when the pre-war oval rear window was replaced by a larger one. This meant reducing the depth of the cooling louvres above the rear engine cover. In 1961 came more radical modifications, though externally the car remained unchanged. The 77 by 64 mm bore and stroke were retained, but the air-cooled flat-four engine was extensively redesigned, resulting in a 13 per cent increase in power. This increased top speed to 72 mph (115 km/h). Bottom gear received synchromesh at the same time. Improvements continued to be made every year: for example in 1965 the windscreen size was increased by 19 per cent, while the side windows were deepened and slimmer window pillars used.

In 1961 Nordhoff's one-model car policy ended with the arrival of the Type 3 1500 with a Beetle-inspired rear-mounted air-cooled flat-four engine and backbone chassis. (The Beetle was Type 1 in Volkswagen factory parlance, while the Type 2 was the popular Transporter light commercial derivative of 1950.) The Type 3 lasted until 1973 but the 2.3 million produced amounted, in Volkswagen terms, to a comparative failure.

Until 1965 the only engine available was the 1200 cc introduced in 1954. But there was another body variant. The Karmann Ghia version, using the Export chassis as its basis, was initiated by Volkswagen in 1953. Styling was by the Italian company Carrozzeria Ghia of Turin, the distinctive lines being the work of Luigi Segre, the firm's owner. He scaled down the one-off *D'Elègance*, designed by Virgil Exner, which his firm had built for Chrysler in 1952, and gave it a new front. Built by the Karmann company from 1955, the model was, in essence, a poor man's Porsche, offering the looks of a sports coupé but without its cost, complications or performance. Top speed was 72 mph (115 km/h), which was superior to the standard Beetle's because of the coupé's better aerodynamics.

At first the Karmann Ghia was available only in left-hand drive form, the right-hand drive variant not appearing until 1960. In 1958 a convertible Karmann Ghia was offered. The 1960 cars were updated and are easily identified by their larger frontal air intakes. Thereafter the Karmann Ghia was to benefit from increases in engine capacity as the Beetle developed, and the model remained in production until 1974.

The next changes to the mainstream Beetle came on the 1966 model, with the introduction of a supplementary 1300 car, virtually identical to the 1200 but with a 1300 badge on its engine lid. The 1285 cc had been achieved by fitting the crankshaft from the Type 3 1500 model, which raised the stroke from 64 to 69 mm. With this larger engine the 1300 Beetle could achieve about 75 mph (120 km/h). Another variant appeared for 1967 with the introduction of a 1500, the enlarged capacity being achieved by retaining the crankshaft from the 1300 but fitting new 83 mm cylinders. This increased capacity to 1493 cc and top speed to 80 mph (128 km/h).

In 1970 another new model was introduced, representing the first radical departure from Porsche's pre-war design. The 1302 series is easily distinguished by its bulbous bonnet, designed to meet criticism of the Beetle's small boot. The transverse torsion bars, with their intrusive beam, were replaced by more compact MacPherson struts. This change, combined with an enlarged bonnet, increased carrying capacity by 85 per cent. At the rear, the cheap swing axle was replaced by a more sophisticated semi-trailing arm layout, as pioneered on a semi-automatic version of the 1500. This was intended to improve road holding, which had been criticised in the United States.

The increase in capacity to 1584 cc represented the limit of the production Beetle engine. This enlargement had been required by the American market, as the de-toxing equipment demanded by the new transatlantic exhaust-emission regulations so stifled performance that an

There were minor changes at the back of the car for 1962, when new rear lights were fitted, which continued until 1967. An exterior driving mirror was introduced at the same time. This is a 1964 right-hand drive British Beetle.

A 1966 1300 model. A '1300' badge was fitted to the engine lid though the model was distinguished by its new wheels with ventilating slots and flat-topped hub caps. The 1200 continued with its existing wheels until 1968.

The first major change to Porsche's original pre-war design came with the arrival of the 1302 series for 1971. The front torsion bars were replaced by MacPherson struts, which permitted a larger boot, and the model is identifiable by its bulbous bonnet.

increase in capacity was necessary to maintain the *status quo*. The bore size was again enlarged, this time to 85 mm, and a new two-port cylinder head was used, as pioneered on the Type 3 1600, making possible speeds of 80 mph (128 km/h).

For 1973 the ultimate version of the car was introduced, the 1303. This was mechanically similar to the 1302 but with a new, more deeply curved windscreen and shorter bonnet. The rear wings were also widened to accommodate distinctive enlarged rear lamps. The 1303 range was available with both 1300 cc and 1600 cc engines but was sold only until 1975.

The Beetle had passed its sales peak after two decades of phenomenal demand. The German factory produced a million Beetles in one year for the first time in 1965, and this total was reached again in 1968, 1969 (when production peaked at 1,076,897), 1970 and 1971. Thereafter, German output fell every

A further Beetle variant for 1973 was the 1303, with a new curved windscreen. The bonnet was accordingly shorter. The rear wings were also widened to accept new enlarged rear lights.

Below the surface of the 1302. These are the more compact Mac-Pherson struts, which were an improvement on the intrusive transverse torsion bars.

On 17th February 1972 the 15,007,034th Beetle was completed, so breaking the 45-year Model T Ford production record. On the right is Rudolph Leiding, who replaced Kurt Lotz as head of Volkswagen in 1971 and remained at Wolfsburg until 1975.

21

The 1200 continued to evolve and from 1976 was the sole Beetle model. This is the 1200L, with chrome bumpers containing the indicators. There was also a more basic 1200A variant.

year, for the Beetle was beginning to show its age. Heinz Nordhoff had died in 1968 and the factory stopped for a minute of silent tribute. His replacement, Kurt Lotz, saw the Beetle-inspired Type 4 into production in 1968, with its rear-mounted air-cooled engine. Wolfsburg's first four-door car was an ungainly model, however, and only some 400,000 were built before production ceased in 1974. Volkswagen tried again in 1970 with the front-wheel drive K70, a design inherited when it bought NSU in 1969. But sales of 211,151 were disappointing and the model was discontinued in 1975.

Despite these relative failures, the Beetle continued to break manufacturing records. On 17th February 1972, the 15,007,034th car left the Wolfsburg production line, so breaking the 45-year-old record, held by the Model T Ford of 1908 to 1927, as the most popular car ever. (Ford then discovered that it had underestimated the Model T production figures and revised the total to 16.5 million, a figure which the Beetle surpassed in 1973.)

However, German Beetle production fell dramatically from 895,801 in 1973 to 451,800 in 1974, a year in which the seemingly impossible happened — Volkswagen recorded a DM807 million (£142.5 million) loss, the first in its history. Part of the reason for this was the Arab-Israeli war of 1973 and the oil price increase, which resulted in a downturn of the German economy. Then, in May 1974, Volkswagen announced the new design that Germany was waiting for, the front-wheel drive Golf. Beetle manufacture ceased at Wolfsburg in July 1974 as the Golf, its true successor, moved into production.

Although Wolfsburg stopped building the Beetle, German output continued at Volkswagen's Emden factory, opened in 1964, to serve the all-important American market. Production continued there until noon on 19th January 1978, when the last German-built Beetle saloon left the production line. Karmann continued to produce the cabriolet Beetle until 10th January 1980, when after forty years the building of Beetles in Germany ceased.

The Beetle and its successor: an early post-war Volkswagen passes a brand-new Golf in Munich.

The Volkswagen factory at Wolfsburg is the largest car factory in the world under one roof. The building in the centre of the photograph, and at right angles to the plant, is the administrative block, while the power station on the extreme right serves both the factory and the town of Wolfsburg.

Ben Pon from Holland, third from left, took delivery of the first Volkswagens to be officially exported from Wolfsburg in October 1947, when the factory was still operating under British control. Pon had ordered six cars but one failed to reach the required standard. Note the chrome bumpers and hub caps, in contrast to the standard model.

THE BEETLE ABROAD

When the Volkswagen was being designed by Porsche in the 1930s, an export version with right-hand drive had been contemplated. It was designated Type 66 in the Stuttgart bureau's design register though none was built. It was not until after the war that exporting began, initially of left-hand drive cars, and in 1947 Ben Pon, a Dutchman, became Volkswagen's first overseas agent. When Heinz Nordhoff took over as Volkswagen's general manager, he immediately identified the United States as the Beetle's most significant export market. Nordhoff sent Ben Pon to New York in January 1949, but the curious car he brought with him generated little interest. Nordhoff subsequently crossed the Atlantic himself and, instead of taking a car, showed photographs. As a result Max Hoffman, who ran a thriving New York agency for European cars, took on Volkswagen's American franchise.

In 1953, however, Volkswagen took back the administration of American sales, and Volkswagen of America was established in 1955, though plans to manufacture the Beetle at a former Studebaker factory were discarded. That year 32,662 Beetles were sold in the USA. Sales then began to rise, aided by a subtle advertising campaign ('I don't want an imported car. I want a Volkswagen.') and the arrival in 1959 of the dynamic Carl Hahn, who remained there until 1964. He subsequently became chairman of the board of management, the head of Volkswagen. When Hahn took over American operations, the Bug, as the car is known in the United States, had been the country's top-selling imported car for four years. In 1959 sales stood at a record 120,442. By 1968, when Beetle sales peaked in America, 423,008 were sold. The Bug had made its mark with the American student population, from whom it elicited a near-fanatical following; but the car also appealed to parents who wanted a second car to complement their own 'gas guzzler'. The Volkswagen remained the country's top-selling imported car until 1975, when it was overtaken by the Toyota Corolla from Japan. In 1978 the Beetle was

Although Ben Pon initially had little success when he tried to sell the Beetle to the Americans in 1949, two decades later the car had attained immense popularity. In 1968 nearly half a million Americans bought Beetles. It was still a small car by American standards, as this 1972 photograph, taken against the Manhattan skyline, clearly shows.

The Beetle-based rear-engined Formula Vee single-seater was created in the United States in 1962 but subsequently spread to Europe. This is Gerhard Mitter, a celebrated European hill-climb champion, at the wheel of a Formula Vee car in 1965, when such vehicles were rare in Europe. The Volkswagen's torsion-bar suspension is readily apparent.

25

withdrawn from the American market and replaced by the Golf, called the Rabbit there, but which never attained the popularity of its predecessor.

By no stretch of the imagination could the Beetle be considered to have sporting or racing pretensions, though Porsche had created a *KdF-Wagen*-based sports coupé to compete in the 1939 Berlin to Rome motor race, an event which was thwarted by the outbreak of the Second World War. The car was, however, the basis of the Porsche marque 356, which appeared in 1948 and was based on Volkswagen mechanical components, though with distinctive and very sporting coupé bodywork.

In 1962, however, American enthusiasts created Formula Vee, which was to prove immensely popular for the next fifteen or so years. In 1958 Hubert L. Brunage, a Volkswagen distributor from Jacksonville, Florida, conceived the idea of a Volkswagen-based racing car which he could run in Formula Junior events. He commissioned Erico Nardi, an Italian engineer based in Turin, to design a prototype, which was built there by Motto and then transported to the United States in 1959. The concept was developed by Colonel George A. Smith, who had retired from the air force and was active within the Sports Car Club of America. He and Bill Duckworth, his business partner, using the Nardi car as a prototype, in 1961 founded Formcar Constructors Incorporated in Orlando, Florida, to produce 1200 cc Volkswagen-based single-seater racers, selling them for $1000 (£355) in kit form and complete for $2400 (£854). It was Smith who conceived the name Formula Vee (for Volkswagen).

Such was the popularity of Formula Vee in the USA that in 1967 Volkswagen, which had been watching from the sidelines, became more directly involved and appointed a competitions manager. The following year Volkswagen of America estimated that there were two thousand Formula Vees there, the work of thirteen manufacturers. In 1967 Volkswagen in Germany initiated Formula Vee Europe, which soon attained a popular following.

The idea was developed in 1970 when Volkswagen of America established the Super Vee Formula, made possible by the arrival in 1968 of the Type 4 Volkswagen with a 1600 cc Beetle-inspired engine. With less constrained chassis and suspension design, higher speeds were possible. The Formula Vee racing car had been capable of 120 mph (193 km/h) but the larger engine could achieve 140 mph (225 km/h).

Both formulas had declined in popularity by the end of the 1970s, although Volkswagen of America endeavoured to keep the Super Vee alive by introducing the water-cooled engine from the Beetle's successor, the Rabbit. Initially, however, the decision to stop selling the Beetle in the United States in 1978 spelt the end of the formula.

Another significant, though more questionable, Beetle variation was initiated in the USA in 1963. A Californian Volkswagen enthusiast, Bruce Meyers, fitted a glass-fibre body on to a shortened Beetle floor pan and produced the Beach Buggy. This concept never received official factory recognition, however.

The USA was the largest market for Volkswagens outside Europe, but in 1953 the company established its first factory outside Germany, in Brazil. The plant at Sao Paulo became the largest Volkswagen factory other than Wolfsburg. Initially Beetles were imported in kit form, the first entirely Brazilian-built car not appearing until 1959. In 1960 Beetle became the market leader in Brazil and ten years later the millionth car left the Sao Paulo production line. Such was the demand in the 1970s that Brazil built its 5 millionth Beetle in 1979. From that year some Brazilian-built 1300 models were converted to run on locally grown sugar cane and are identified by an 'Alcool' badge on their engine lids. In 1980 Brazil introduced its own model, the Gol, with a front-mounted 1300 Beetle engine. Brazil continued to build the Beetle proper until 1986 but the economic problems of the country, with resulting heavy company losses, led to Volkswagen combining its operation there with Ford in 1987, though the resulting Autolatina company is still a formidable force within the Brazilian market and exports the Audi-engined Volkswagen Fox to the USA, where it

From 1953 the Beetle was assembled in Brazil from kits supplied from Germany and production proper did not begin until 1959. This 1200 dates from that year. The distinctive bumpers were fitted to protect the front of the Beetle from larger, higher and more substantial American cars.

The Volkswagen plant in Sao Paulo, Brazil, was the largest Volkswagen factory outside Germany. In 1987 the company merged its Brazilian operations with those of Ford.

The Beetle-based, Packard-inspired glass-fibre bodied Madison of 1980 was available in kit form from GP Vehicles of Isleworth, Middlesex, or it could be supplied ready to drive. It was subsequently taken over by Madison Sportscars of West Kingsdown, Kent, and remained in production until about 1993.

effectively replaces the Beetle.

Brazil was also responsible for servicing Volkswagen of Nigeria, established near Ojo on the Lagos to Badagri highway in 1975. Initially 1300 and 1500 cars were produced, using kits, but Beetle production ceased in 1986 when Sao Paulo discontinued the model. The first Beetle built in South Africa was completed at Uitenhage in 1951, and manufacturing continued there until 18th January 1979, just under a year after the last Beetle left Volkswagen's Emden production line.

Britain received Beetles direct from Wolfsburg, though from 1961 cars were also imported from Volkswagen's Belgian factory. Sales had begun unofficially in 1948, when John Colborne-Baber sold second-hand Beetles from his garage at Ripley, Surrey. Sales were placed on an official footing in 1953 when VW Motors was established, though Nordhoff decided that the company should be British-owned to avoid any anti-German feeling. By 1957 the Beetle had become Britain's top-selling imported car and built up a loyal following. It remained so until 1972, when Type 3 sales fell.

Although Germany stopped building Beetles in 1978, the European market, including Germany itself, Austria, Italy and Holland, was supplied with left-hand drive cars from Volkswagen's Mexican factory. This had been established in 1964, when production of the 1200 Beetle began, and it is this model, with minor improvements,

that the Pueblo plant produced from that date. The 1600 Beetle was also made there for a time, though this was for the Mexican rather than the export market.

On 15th May 1981 the 20 millionth Beetle was produced in Mexico. Accordingly, the Mexican factory produced a special version, the Silver Bug, with '20 Millionen' displayed on the engine cover, gear-lever knob and key fob. Mexico also continued to supply the European market until 1986.

On 24th June 1992 the 21 millionth Beetle was built in Mexico. And fourteen months later, on 23rd August 1993, amazingly, the model was reintroduced in Brazil after a seven-year hiatus, at the suggestion of the country's president, Beetle enthusiast Itamar Franco. The revived 1.6 litre car, available in alcohol and petrol-fuelled guises, was destined to survive for over three years, with production ceasing in December 1996. That really was the end of the Brazilian Beetle.

Mexico was still going strong, however, and in 1994 it had updated its Beetle's engine, which was converted to run on unleaded petrol, was fuel-injected and fitted with a catalytic converter. Two versions are built, the no-frills City and the Classico, the latter being offered with a range of metallic paints, and front disc brakes. An open version is also produced but the Escarabajo is not like the old European cabriolet because it retains the saloons' doors.

These are left-hand-drive cars but the

This 1200 model is pictured in Thailand in 1965. Beetle assembly plants in the Far East were located in the Philippines, Malaysia and Singapore.

model is available in Britain with right-hand steering although, it should be stressed, this is not an official conversion.

The New Beetle has been produced in Mexico since 1997. Although it is visually related to the original, it does not share a mechanical alliance because it is built on the platform of Volkswagen's current best-selling front-wheel-drive Golf. It is therefore powered by a front-located water-cooled engine rather than an air-cooled rear-mounted one. However, the Golf underpinning has brought criticism of the packaging, particularly for rear-seat passengers.

The New Beetle originated as a concept car that was unveiled to a phenomenal response at the 1994 Detroit Auto Show. It was the brainchild of J. Carroll Mays, VW's head of styling at its Design Center at Simi Valley, California, so located to monitor trends on the all-important American market. The yellow Concept 1 saloon was joined at the Geneva Motor Show of the same year by the open Concept Cabrio.

The idea was not given corporate approval until November 1994, when Wolfsburg began work to transform the one-off saloon into a production model.

Mexico was chosen to build it and the adjacent United States market targeted for its launch. There it was hoped that potential customers, or their parents, would recall the legendary heyday of the Bug in the 1960s.

Two versions of the New Beetle, which, unlike Concept 1, is a hatchback, were initially on offer with a choice of a 2 litre petrol engine or a 1.9 litre diesel one. Capable in the former guise of 110 mph (177 km/h), it was launched at the Detroit Auto Show in January 1998. Continental Europe followed in November although Britain and Japan, which required right-hand-drive cars, did not receive their New Beetles until 2000.

At the time of writing (2003), a cabriolet version is promised although it remains to be seen whether the new Beetle will experience anything like the longevity of the original. It is still in production but its position as the most popular car in the history of the automobile was challenged in June 2002 by the completion of the 21,517,415th in-house Golf, although this does differ significantly from the 1974 original. Nevertheless, success clearly breeds success!

The Silver Bug, produced in Mexico to commemorate the manufacture of the 20 millionth Beetle on 15th May 1981, with Volkswagen's own pre-production VW38 of 1938 in the foreground.

Left: *The 1200 Beetle under construction at Volkswagen's Mexican plant, opened in 1964 and in 1989 the only factory in the world to manufacture the Beetle. This photograph was taken in 1970.*

Mexico produced this special model in 1987, to celebrate the fiftieth anniversary of the Beetle's creation. It has a commemorative badge on the front wing and the sports wheels that appeared on many special-edition models from 1972 onwards.

A New Beetle of 2002. In 2003 it was available in six versions: 1.6 litre, 1.9 TDI PD, 2.0 litre, 1.8T – all with four-cylinder engines; the V five-cylinder V5, and the V5 Sport Edition, which is capable of over 140 mph (225 km/h).

FURTHER READING

The following list includes some older books that may be found in second-hand bookshops, libraries or autojumbles.

Etzold, Hans-Rudiger. *The Beetle: The Chronicles of the People's Car* (volumes 1, 2 and 3). Haynes, 1985.
Fry, Robin. *The VW Beetle*. David & Charles, 1980.
Hopfinger, K. B. *Beyond Expectation*. G. T. Foulis, 1954 and 1971.
Post, Dan R. *Volkswagen Nine Lives Later*. Horizon House, 1966 and 1986.
Seume, Keith. *The Beetle*. Bramley Books, 1997.
Seume, Keith. *Millennium Bug*. Motorbooks International, 2000.
Wood, Jonathan. *VW Beetle, A Collector's Guide*. Motor Racing Publications, 1983, 1987, 1989, 1995 and 1997.
Wood, Jonathan. *The New Beetle*. Bramley Books, 1999.

JOURNALS

VW Motoring, Warners Group, The Maltings, West Street, Bourne, Lincolnshire PE10 9PH. Telephone: 01778 391000. Website: www.vmonline.co.uk
Volkswagen Driver, Autometrix Publications, Campion House, 1 Greenfield Road, Westoning, Bedfordshire MK45 5JD. Telephone: 01525 750500. Website: www.autometrix.co.uk Mostly modern.
VolksWorld, IPC Focus Network, Focus House, Dingwall Avenue, Croydon, Surrey CR9 2TA. Telephone: 020 8774 0600. Website: www.volksworld.com

CLUBS

There is no shortage of clubs for the Beetle enthusiast. Details of your nearest one can be obtained from the *Association of British VW Clubs*: John Daniel, 76 Eastfield Road, Burnham, Buckinghamshire SL1 7PF. Telephone: 01628 604254. Website: www.abvwc.org.uk
The Historic Volkswagen Club. Rod Sleigh, 28 Longnor Road, Brooklands, Telford, Shropshire TF1 3NY. Website: www.historicvws.org.uk All pre-1968 Volkswagens
The Volkswagen Owners' Club of Great Britain, PO Box 7, Burntwood, Staffordshire WS7 8SB. Owners of all Volkswagens.
The Volkswagen Cabriolet Owners' Club GB, Phil Cushway, 2 Hope Mount, Upperwood Road, Matlock Bath, Derbyshire DE4 3PD. Website: www.beetlecabrio.co.uk
Karmann Ghia Owners' Club, John Figg, 13 Hilltop Road, Toms Lane, Kings Langley, Hertfordshire WD4 8NS.

PLACES TO VISIT

Museum displays may be altered and readers are advised to check before travelling that the relevant vehicles are on show and to ascertain the opening times. An up-to-date listing of all road-transport museums in the United Kingdom can be found on www.motormuseums.com

GREAT BRITAIN

Haynes Motor Museum, Sparkford, Yeovil, Somerset BA22 7LH. Telephone: 01963 440804. Website www.haynesmotormuseum.co.uk
National Motor Museum, Beaulieu, Brockenhurst, Hampshire SO4 7ZN. Telephone: 01590 612345. Website: www.beaulieu.co.uk
Science Museum, Exhibition Road, South Kensington, London SW7 2DD. Telephone: 0870 870 4771. Website: www.sciencemuseum.org.uk

GERMANY

Autostadt gmbh, Stadtbrücke, 38440 Wolfsburg. Volkswagen's own collection. Website: www.autostadt.de/english
Porsche Museum, Porschestrasse 42, 70435 Stuttgart-Zuffenhausen, Baden-Würtemberg. This has a Volkswagen section.